AF375501

This is a work of fiction. All characters, events portrayed in this book are either products of the author's imagination or are used fictitiously.

Benny and Friends say...Manners Matter!

Illustrations by Nara Joyce Lee
Book Design and Publication by Green Avenue Books & Publishing LLC

Printed in the United States of America

ISBN 9798869044730

Written & illustrated by Nara Joyce Lee

Benny & Friends say...
Manners Matter!

Benny the Elephant says...

"Hello!"

"Ahn-young!"
안녕

"Ni-hao!"
你好

Ronnie the Rabbit says...

"Please."

"Joo-sae-yo."
주세요.

"Qîng."
请

5

Bobby the Polar Bear says...

"Thank you!"

"Gamsa-bap-ni-da!"
감사합니다!

"Xièxiè!"
谢谢

7

Luna the Llama says...

"Thank you for the meal."

"Jal-muk-get-ssem-ni-da."
잘먹겠습니다.

"xièxiè shíwù"
谢谢食物

Chonky the Monkey says...

"Yummy!"

"Ma-shi-da!"
맛있다!

"Hào chi!"
好吃

11

Lamby the Baby Lamb says...

"Excuse me!"

"Shil-lae-hap-ni-da!"
실례합니다!

"Duìbuqǐ."
对不起!

Crunchy the Carrot says...

"I'm sorry!"

"Jwae-song-hap-ni-da!"
죄송합니다!

"Duìbuqǐ."
对不起!

Sammy the Sloth Says...

"Goodnight!"

"Ahn-Young-he-joo-moo-sae-yo."
안녕히 주무세요.

"Wǎn'ān."
晚安

About the Author

Nara Lee is a Korean American who was born in Seoul, South Korea but grew up in the Bay Area of California. She went to School at the Art Institute of Chicago studying Film, Video, and New Media as well as Art Therapy. Nara is currently a full time mommy to a beautiful baby boy and two fur pups, video producer, and holds the title of Miss Boise Metro of Idaho. Mother to a half Korean and half Taiwanese baby boy, Jordan, Nara was motivated to keep both cultures and languages available for her baby at all times. As she was in search of multilingual books, found that there weren't many available, especially to kids who are trilingual. For Jordan's first birthday, she made it a mission to illustrate and write a book where he can learn English, Korean, and Chinese and the different cultures' etiquette while making it fun to find his favorite stuffed friends in his book! Nara hopes that with this book being available to other parents, families, and communities with diverse backgrounds can find ease in educating little ones of language and cultures.